1994

WRITE FOR SUCCESS

**Preparing a Successful
Professional School Application**

Evelyn W. Jackson, Ph.D.

Harold R. Bardo, Ph.D.

MEDPREP
School of Medicine
Southern Illinois University

Published by
The National Association of Advisors
for the Health Professions, Inc.
P.O. Box 5017 Station A
Champaign, IL 61820-9017

June 1987
Second Printing, February 1988

Typesetting donated by BAR/BRI Professional Testing Centers.

Printed in Champaign, Illinois

Published by:

The National Association of Advisors for the Health Professions, Inc.

ISBN 0-911899-02-2

CONTENTS

Foreword 1

Introduction 3

Open-ended Application Essays 5

What Can You Write About? 7

Evolution of an Essay 11

Sample Essays 17

What Impression Does Your Essay Convey? 21

Supplemental Applications 35

Conclusion 37

ACKNOWLEDGEMENTS

This monograph is possible because of all we have learned from working with our students. Thus we wish to thank many MEDPREP students who wrote and rewrote and rewrote at our suggestion. As they learned, so did we.

We are also grateful to the admissions officers who volunteered to share their impressions of the various essays. They are Billy Rankin at Baylor Medical College, Houston, TX; Norma Wagoner at the University of Cincinnati College of Medicine, Cincinnati, OH; and Daniel Burr, Loyola University of Chicago Stritch School of Medicine, Chicago, IL.

FOREWORD

Writing is a necessary skill. Most of us spend several years of our educational lives in language arts classes that are devoted in part to writing. Yet many of us find it difficult to write clearly. The purpose of this monograph is not to teach you how to write in a general sense. It is instead geared specifically to help you write clearly for tasks related to the health professions application process. Suggestions, strategies, and examples will be provided that will help you write clearly. The importance of writing clearly must not be underestimated.

For example, some researchers and admissions committees report that among candidates who meet minimum admissions criteria for medical school, factors other than GPA and MCAT scores are more important to the admissions committee than those numbers combined. If a substantial portion of the variability in admissions is accounted for by factors other than quantitative measures, more attention should be given to those "other" factors. Our experience has been that applicants do not give enough attention to the factors other than GPA and admissions test scores when they prepare their applications. More attention should be given to one of those other factors and that is the ability to write clearly. This monograph has been written to help you with the writing tasks of the professional school application process.

Since our experience has been with pre-medical students, the examples that we've selected have come from the applications that are part of the medical school application process. While considerable attention is directed to the AMCAS application, it is safe to assume that the advice is applicable to preparing the written portions of any health professions application, including the Association of American Dental Schools Application System (AADSAS) and the American Association of Colleges of Osteopathic Medicine Application Service (AACOMAS).

INTRODUCTION

Although this monograph will specifically discuss the writing tasks related to the professional school application process, there are other suggestions for enhancing your application that will be considered first. The application is often your initial contact with a school, and first meetings are often those where lasting impressions are made. As a consequence, you should strive to make the best impression possible. The application process is not unlike the face-to-face interview with a prospective employer. The interviewee often makes a special effort to learn as much as possible about the employer. Such efforts may include researching the history of the organization, reading the company's latest quarterly reports, and learning where the company stands in relation to its competition. Should the opportunity arise, the interviewee will not miss the chance to demonstrate to the interviewer a more than passing interest in the company.

Suggestion #1: *Investigate Schools Before Applying*

You should be serious about attending any school to which you apply. It is not wise to apply to schools simply because there is no application fee. An applicant would do well to consider a school for some of the same reasons a person chooses a place of employment. The overriding reason for applying to a medical school should be more than simply to obtain a seat in any school. The applicant should have some method of reducing medical schools to an appropriate number. This reduction will give the applicant a stake in the process. The additional work required to make the applicant a good candidate will be easier for him or her. Since the first step in the application process is to reduce the number of schools to a workable number, the applicant must investigate thoroughly all schools of interest.

Suggestion #2: *Restrain Use of the Unusual in the Process*

Sometimes schools request a photograph to accompany the application. One creative applicant responded to the request by drawing a sketch of himself; he was not accepted. If a photograph is requested, choose one that best represents you. A photograph taken in fraternity or sorority apparel or one taken while in bars or on vacation at a tropical resort is not considered appropriate. Thus, you should be dressed conservatively to project a professional image. This photograph should represent you as a serious applicant to medical school.

Suggestion #3: *Consider Readers of Your Application*

You should consider who is going to read your application. Admissions committees are usually composed of persons who are proud to be associated with the profession and as such are gatekeepers of the profession. This gatekeeping function is especially apparent today with the concerns of malpractice. Many admissions committees, in a word, are conservative. Thus, you would do well to reserve the creative and unusual for other endeavors. Our experience has been that a cleverly written application will receive a chuckle or two, but seldom will it receive serious consideration.

Suggestion #4: *Read Before You Write*

Exercise caution by reading questions raised in the application before answering them. All too often, applicants respond to questions that are not asked, and do not respond appropriately to questions raised. The space allowed for the response to questions is often limited. Admissions committees have large numbers of applications to review and usually seek to determine how appropriately and succinctly each applicant responds to the question in the space provided.

On the other hand, the application often has space for additional comments, and the applicant may be asked to respond to specific questions in this section. In other applications, such response is optional. We believe that if this option is available, the applicant should respond and take advantage of the opportunity to establish additional linkages with the admissions committee.

Suggestion #5: *Correct Obvious Errors*

If you make a favorable impression on paper, you will increase your chances of getting to the interview stage. It is surprising how many applicants wait to apply until shortly before the deadline. Completed in a hurry, many applications suffer from obvious, correctable errors. Your applications should be typed, error-free, and as aesthetically appealing as possible.

Of course, there also must be substance in the application. If your application is free of typos, smudges, misspelled words, and other unappealing characteristics, the readers will look carefully at the substance of the application. In other words, you should not expect an admissions committee to struggle trying to read an illegible, handwritten application. Your application is your first and often your only link to the admissions committee. It should represent your best effort.

Suggestion #6: *Organize*

Applying to professional school entails a lot of paperwork. You will have an easier time managing the flow of paper if you are organized. Create a file for the AMCAS, AADSAS or AACOMAS application and each school to which you are applying. Prepare a schedule or time line that will permit you to keep track of due dates for the secondary or supplemental applications. Create one master chart which allows you to lay out all the requirements of each school's application. The chart will provide an overall view of how you're managing all the details. Photocopy everything before you place it in the mail. Keep all of your application materials in one place; an expandable accordion-type folder that can be closed works well.

OPEN-ENDED APPLICATION ESSAYS

It is a common practice in professional school applications to present the applicant with a blank page, or half-page, as an opportunity for the student to reveal something about himself/herself to the members of the admissions committee. Since our experience has been with pre-medical students we have directed our suggestions to the preparation of the AMCAS Personal Comments page.

Again, an applicant to any health professions school should find the information useful in the context of his/her chosen profession.

The AMCAS application is a four-page form, three-fourths of which provides medical schools with factual information about your family background and academic history. The remaining page, consisting of 75 square inches of blank space, provides an opportunity for you to make a statement to the admissions committee(s) of the schools to which you are applying.

The page is titled, "For Personal Comments," and the directions in the instruction booklet state:

> You should be aware that many admissions committees place significant weight on your personal comments as it assists them in developing a greater understanding of you as an individual.

> To obtain maximum use of this space, you should provide additional information which you wish to be considered in the evaluation of your application, as well as amplifying or explaining answers given elsewhere on the form, *i.e.,* you may use this space to elaborate on your responses to Questions 9-14 of the AMCAS Application. Any words and/or sentences that extend beyond the black lines provided as boundaries for the text of your personal comments will not appear on the copy of your application being sent to designated medical schools. Pictures and other materials attached to the application will not be reproduced. Do not enclose additional personal comments or materials such as resumes or curriculum vitae. They will delay the processing of your application and may be returned to you. *Your personal comments must not exceed the space provided.* Supplemental pages of the AMCAS Application cannot be used to continue your personal comments.

While the information in the instruction booklet is important and you need to abide by the guidelines, the above paragraphs are almost as important for what they do not say as what they do say. While it is clear that you may not exceed the limits of the page, there is no recommendation made as to how much to write. Note that you are not given much direction about what to say on the page; you are left to your own devices to structure a statement.

Most applicants to medical school use the space to discuss their motivation for a career in medicine, their experiences which have contributed to their preparation for studying medicine and their goals for the future. Essays vary in length; one-half to three-quarters of the page might be considered average.

As you decide what to write, create an outline which denotes the main topics you want to discuss. The outline should permit you to develop paragraphs which are organized and succinct.

How can you know if you have written well? Our best advice is that you let someone who is a good writer read your essay and give you feedback regarding the quality of your writings. It is advisable to solicit help from someone who will not be concerned about hurting your feelings and who understands the purpose of the essay.

Some of the most valuable feedback that your reader can provide comes in the form of questions that are raised when your essay is read. If your writing is not clear your reader may not be sure what you're saying. Thus, not only is your message lost, you have made a negative impression about your ability to communicate clearly. Speak directly to your reader—let him/her understand without having to struggle to make sense of what you've said.

If you want to be your own reader on the first drafts allow some time to lapse before you read your own writing. Put your essay away for a couple of days and then, when you read it, follow this procedure: (1) read it aloud to yourself, and (2) listen carefully to what you hear. You need to determine that you have said what you meant. If you stumble over your reading or a sentence or phrase sounds awkward that's a clue that you need to revise.

WHAT CAN YOU WRITE ABOUT?

You might choose to write about your motivation for a career in medicine. It is likely that you will be asked during an interview why you want to be a physician. The Personal Comments page is an opportunity for you to begin dealing with the question.

First, think about it carefully. Mull it over before you write so that you can put something down on paper. For some students, the hardest part is getting started. We concede that starting may be difficult, but if you understand that *what you write will be rewritten or revised,* it might make it easier to begin.

You may be an individual who enjoys writing, who writes well, and who has had a lot of writing experience. You will have an easier time with this application process, and you will find that you do not need some of the advice we share.

On a sheet of paper write your response to the question: Why do you want to be a physician?

Once you have drafted an answer, consider the next question: What other occupation or profession can provide what you say you want out of being a physician?

For example, if you had written something about enjoying people and wanting to help them, you need to realize that a produce clerk in a grocery store could make the same statement.

Indeed, why do you want to be a physician? If you find this difficult to answer, think through the following questions as an exercise in focusing your thoughts:

Why don't you want to be a teacher?

Why don't you want to be a nurse?

Why don't you want to be a produce clerk in a grocery store?

Why don't you want to be a research scientist?

Your answers to the above questions may help you to better understand what it may mean to be a physician. If you find that you are still at a loss to define why you want to be a physician, that is a clue that you need to re-examine your choice of medicine as a career.

Extracurricular Activities and Work Experience

Another topic you may consider is your background of experiences. You listed honors and awards, extracurricular activities, and employment history on the first page of the AMCAS application. Be sure this is done *before* you begin writing. It is not necessary, nor desirable, for you to repeat the details of these experiences on the Personal Comments page. Your reader has the information on page one if he/she wants it. Limit your references to dates, names, and places. Your reader may be distracted by the details and not pay attention when you do say something meaningful.

To help you develop your statement about your background and experiences, think about answers to the following questions:

What did you learn from your extracurricular activities or work experiences?

If you had a leadership role, how did you contribute to getting the job done?

How have you matured as a result of these experiences?

We suggest that you describe your experiences so that your reader can conclude that you are mature, independent, etc., but do not recommend that you use those adjectives in your discussion. You want your reader to develop an impression of you independently.

If you have volunteered or worked in a health-care setting and you find that you are writing that you know what it means to be a physician, be aware that you may give your reader an impression of being naive. Avoid getting ahead of yourself. You're not expected to know what it means to be a physician. It is reasonable, however, for the schools to expect that you have undertaken some investigation of medicine and that you can communicate these insights in a well-written statement.

Irregularities in Your Academic Record

Your academic record is outlined in detail on pages 3 and 4 of the AMCAS application. While there are some academic records that merit attention on the Personal Comments page, most do not. Most applicants to medical school have what we call very traditional-looking academic records. See Figure 1 for a sample.

The information required on pages 3 and 4 may reveal what we call "academic irregularities" if they are in your academic history. According to the guidelines in the instruction booklet, you must identify whether you have withdrawals (W) from any courses or whether you have any incompletes (I) for courses on your official transcript(s). You are also to label any courses you have repeated (R). These (W, R, and/or I) are noted as academic irregularities because they reflect that something interfered with your being able to satisfactorily complete the course in one term.

If you have more than a couple of any one of the irregularities indicated on your academic record, you need to consider addressing them in your Personal Comment. When you write, you want to give your reader an explanation, not an excuse. At the very least, you should acknowledge the situation and give your reader some indication of what you are doing about it. Remember, it's okay to have made mistakes. It is also reasonable to expect that you can acknowledge having made them and tell what you are doing as a result of having learned from them.

Below-Average Grades

Below-average grades may need some explanation. If you repeated the course, the second grade you earned, if average or better, is evidence that you demonstrated satisfactory performance. If you did not repeat a course for which you earned a below-average grade, you might choose to discuss why you did not retake it.

Notice that we've said your below-average grades may need some explanation, not excuses. An entirely different impression is conveyed if you make excuses for your academic performance. Consider the following statement written by a student who wanted to discuss her academic record:

In my response to my attached academic record, I strongly believe that my transcript provides an inadequate superficial view of my accomplishments and, more importantly, my capabilities. For example, during my senior year I received a failing grade in a humanities elective. Upon surveying my academic record, one could very easily assume that this situation was brought about by lackadaisical study habits. However, this assumption is erroneous not only in this case, but in the majority of cases where "D" grades are involved. With regards to the "F," the class grade was based on a single composition which was to be handed in toward the end of the term (after the drop date). Due to a serious illness in the family (my mother contracted double pneumonia), I was forced to leave school. However, I did notify the instructor of my upcoming absence. Once at home, I mailed the assignment post-dated appropriately; however the instructor didn't actually receive the composition until two days later. The composition was penalized for the tardiness and this resulted in my original grade of 86 percent (B+) being reduced to 36 percent (F). Upon my request, the Ombudsman investigated the matter and concluded that since the instructor's syllabus states that all late work will be penalized, that there was nothing he could do. My parents' attempt to speak with the instructor were futile, and since the term was soon coming to a close, the failing grade went on my transcript.

In reference to the other below satisfactory grades, I feel as though there are several causative factors involved. For example, I did not attend a college preparatory high school, thus there was no emphasis on study skills or areas involving BCPM. This, coupled with the fact that I entered college at 16 years of age (which I considered to be a bit premature), played a major role in my first unsuccessful semester. Once I understood this I buckled down my second semester and did very well. I ran into problems in my 3rd semester because of too much emphasis on pledging activities. In general, I've always found that classes of BCPM were more difficult than my other classes and I felt that this was due to my inadequate background. Thus, at this point I attempted to place more emphasis in these areas (BCPM) than in my humanities. These efforts were fruitless also because of my lack of study skills. I felt that lacking in this area was most detrimental to me because I used to spend a lot of time studying but I always felt that I didn't get a lot accomplished. Thus I would "burn out" easily. For example, in the case of the "D's" on my transcript, more often than not, I would go into the final exam with a "B" and end up with a "D." I feel this resulted from a lack of study skills especially with respect to time management. However, I am pleased to say that I have been making progress and will continue to do so until this deficiency is completely eliminated.

This is not only too lengthy and detailed, it also reflects negatively on the student. Most of this recitation of events conveys that something or someone other than this student is responsible for her situation. Medical schools are not interested in applicants who are unrealistic about themselves.

Non-Traditional Background

In our work with pre-meds, we have encountered many non-traditional students who have wanted to make themselves appear to be more like traditional pre-med applicants. They have a tendency to gloss over what sets them apart and try to make themselves fit a mold. This is neither necessary nor desirable. A student may be non-traditional by virtue of race, sex, age, academic background, or life experiences.

If you feel that you are not typical enough, we suggest that you re-think the situation and consider how to turn it into an advantage. For example, you may be in your late 20s or early 30s and feel that you are different from the other applicants because you are so much older. Well, you are older, but you are probably also more mature and more experienced. Your commitment to medicine may appear to be stronger or more sincere if it involves a career change for you.

It is not possible to delineate all the ways an applicant may be non-traditional. No matter what form this difference takes, you need to use it to your advantage. If you have trouble making lemonade out of these so-called lemons, talk it over with someone you trust and who can be a good advisor to you.

Future Plans

One other topic you might want to write about is your long-term goals. We suggest that you devote space to your future plans if you can say something definitive that has some substantial basis. Again, you do not need to write something just because you think the admissions committee wants to read it. If it is insincere, it will not fool anyone. Experienced readers quickly pick up on insincerity and, at the very least, will tune out your message.

EVOLUTION OF AN ESSAY

What is it like to prepare an essay which addresses the questions of why you have chosen the profession and how you are an acceptable applicant?

Before you read the drafts of one student's Personal Comments page, become acquainted with her by reading her final version that was part of a successful application.

Personal Comments—Final Version

My decision to seek a career in medicine was influenced by various work and personal experiences. However, there is one person, very dear to me, who played a significant role in finalizing my career objective, my grandmother. Shortly after my twelfth birthday, she was diagnosed as having meningitis and was hospitalized. I can remember having very intense feelings of frustration resulting from the fact that I was unable to care for her. Five days after she had been admitted into the hospital, she went into a coma. At her bedside, I promised her that I would work as hard as I could to become a doctor so that I could help someone get well so they could return home. When she died the following week, I became even more determined than ever to become a physician in hopes of sparing others.

Over the last nine years my interest in becoming a physician has been strengthened by my extracurricular and work activities. While in high school, I worked as an assistant to a registered pharmacist. My duties consisted of citing pharmacological references which would be incorporated in a monthly newsletter published by the company. As a result of this exposure, I was able to interpret how various drugs could be used to modify the functions of the autonomic nervous system to alleviate illness. During the summer of 1979, I was a volunteer worker at the hospital, where I processed medical histories for incoming patients, took temperatures, and prepared blood and urine specimens. This was my first "hands on" experience and gave me an idea of some of the intricate workings of a hospital.

While at Midwestern University, my participation in extracurricular activities enhanced my interpersonal and leadership skills. They provided situations in which I was allowed to exercise my capabilities as president, vice president, treasurer and secretary.

I have also been involved in other activities which have given me the opportunity to help those who are socioeconomically disadvantaged and unable to care for themselves. This volunteer work ranged from organizing food drives and establishing a tutor program for primary school children to visiting pediatric wards of hospitals and talking with the children to ease their fears that resulted from being hospitalized. These services were rewarding to me personally because I was able to make a positive change in their lives and, in many cases, become a friend to many that really needed some type of role model. I also worked on the crisis hotline at a local hospital. My responsibilities were to be a very attentive, confident listener and provide the caller with reference information pertinent to the inquiry. Through this experience I have gained confidence in dealing with crisis situations.

During my senior year at Midwestern, I was employed by the United States Department of Agriculture as a Biological Aide. I received, cataloged and analyzed the triglyceride content of seeds shipped from various parts of the United States, thus I worked extensively with nuclear magnetic resonance machines and mass spectroscopy equipment. I also performed bioassays on the velvet leaf plant. This experience improved my research ability and familiarized me with agricultural methods of mass production. Presently, I am a volunteer autopsy assistant.

My desire to become a physician is sincere and I am committed to doing whatever is necessary to achieve my goal.

To illustrate some of the advice previously mentioned we are including this student's Personal Comments essay, draft by draft, and readers' comments so that you may see how the essay evolved.

These drafts are more representative of difficulty with content than spelling and other mechanical considerations. Thus the feedback after each paragraph addresses what is said rather than noting grammatical errors.

Personal Comments—First Draft [Three paragraphs: motivation, extracurricular activities and future plans]

> While in pursuit of a career in medicine, I've found that certain personal characteristics will not only facilitate my quest, but are often an integral part of the medical field itself. These characteristics include determination, personal integrity, academic and social discipline, unyielding dedication and a genuine interest in helping others. This latter aspect provides the motivational foundation which encouraged me to pursue a career in medicine, more specifically, pediatrics. I have always had a natural attraction for children, and being employed in a field which benefits them not only proves to be very fulfilling, but provides me with an opportunity to participate in an area of great personal worth.

(Motivation for Medicine—Paragraph #1)

Comment:

Your first paragraph provides no direction for the rest of your essay. There is no focus in the paragraph itself. Your readers know the characteristics required for medical training — if you want to discuss them make your discussion more personal so your reader can learn something about you. As it is, you convey a message in a wordy, cumbersome manner. What do you mean by "natural attraction for children?" Have you enjoyed working with children? Just say so; there's no need to bury your intention in a lot of words.

> During my previous course work at Midwestern University, I was involved in several extracurricular activities. These include holding the office of Vice-President of the Student Advisory Council, the offices of Vice president, Treasurer and social chair person of my sorority, and an active member of the National Technical Association and the Student Alliance. Having been affiliated with these organizations has really been a positive factor in my life because they entailed social interaction with respect to working with others towards a common goal. They also provided an atmosphere in which I was working with others who may or may not have shared my ideas and beliefs. Learning to deal with situations of this nature is vital, since the medical profession involves making judgements and decisions based on your beliefs, for a common purpose.

(Extracurricular activities—Paragraph #2)

Comment:

Your reader is not going to pay attention to the details listed in paragraph 2. Remember, all of this is on the first page of the application; you don't need to repeat it here. Your attempt to link your participation in these activities with medicine is weak. In the last sentence you've omitted any reference to a knowledge base — why? What do you mean by "for a common purpose"?

> Looking toward the future, I would like to begin my career working with a hospital in the department of pediatrics with later intention of opening a private practice. During my stay at the hospital, I would like to hold a position in a governing body, for example, the board of

directors. Also, teaching a class that deals with some clinical and diagnostic aspects of pediatric medicine is of interest to me. However, I would like to pursue this concurrently with my daily hospital work.

(Future Plans—Paragraph #3)

Comment:

This is too general and you're back to a statement of intentions that you started in paragraph 1.

Overall Comment:

Your reader does not learn about you from this personal comment. The points you have tried to address are lost in cumbersome, awkward sentences. Try again. What about your work experience that's mentioned on the first page?

Personal Comments—Second Draft [Four paragraphs: motivation, extracurricular activities, future plans and work experience]

> While in pursuit of a medical career, I've found that certain personal characteristics are vital to one's success in a medical profession. These characteristics include determination, personal integrity, academic and social discipline, unyielding dedication and a genuine interest in helping others. This latter aspect provides the motivational foundation which encouraged me to pursue a career of this nature, specifically, pediatrics. Young children have always fascinated me and being able to work with them in a positive manner would prove to be a most rewarding task.

(Motivation for Medicine—Paragraph #1)

Comment:

You have attempted to simplify this but it doesn't reveal anything meaningful about you. There are still some awkward and/or ambiguous phrases: social discipline, motivational foundation, a career of this nature, in a positive manner (clearly you would not want your work with children to be negative, but it is hard to know exactly what you're talking about).

> During my previous course work at Midwestern University, I was involved in several extracurricular activities. My participation in these organizations has really been a positive factor in my life because they entailed social interaction with respect to working with others toward a common goal. They also provided an atmosphere in which I was working with others who may or may not have shared my ideas and beliefs. Learning to deal with situations of this nature is vital, since the medical profession involves making judgements and decisions based on one's beliefs, for the welfare of others.

(Extracurricular Activities—Paragraph #2)

Comment:

Your reader needs to be able to proceed through your statement without stumbling over what you mean. In the first sentence of this paragraph you have said that your involvement in extracurricular activities was part of your course work at Midwestern University. Is that what you mean?

> Looking toward the future, I would like to become a resident in pediatrics and afterwards establish a private practice. In a later point of my career I would like to hold a position in a governing body, for example, the board of directors. Also, instructing a class that deals with some clinical and diagnostic aspects of pediatric medicine is of interest to me. I would like to pursue this concurrently with my daily hospital duties.

(Future Plans—Paragraph #3)

Comment:

This attraction to the distant future is not important to me (just one of your readers). If you decide to include this it would be more appropriate at the end of your essay.

> With respect to work experience, during the summer of 1982 and over Christmas break of that same year, I was employed at the United States Department of Agriculture. My position was titled "Chemical-Physical Aid." My duties included preparing Esters for samples of Sapium Sebiferous Seeds that were imported from South America and the Gulf of Mexico. Once these esters were prepared, I analyzed the fatty acid composition via mass spectrophotometric machines and nuclear magnetic resonance machines. Other duties included preparing bio-assays of velvet leaf plant. This included synthesizing and processing acetone and water extracts from various seeds and applying them in different dilutions. After a short incubation period, I would analyze them for percent inhibition. I found this work experience very helpful.

(Work Experience—Paragraph #4)

Comment:

This is out of place. Remember, if the details are already available to the reader from the other pages of the application, you don't need to repeat everything. You've taken up most of the paragraph with the details of the position you held—it would be more informative to your reader to talk about what you learned as a result of having had the experience.

Overall Comment:

There is no apparent relationship among your paragraphs and the chronology is poor.

Personal Comments—Third Draft [Two paragraphs: motivation and extracurricular activities]

> While in pursuit of a medical career I've found that certain personal characteristics are vital to one's success in the profession. These characteristics include determination, personal integrity, academic discipline, unyielding dedication and a genuine interest in helping others. This latter aspect provides the motivational foundation which encouraged me to pursue a career in pediatrics. Young children have always fascinated me and being able to care for them would prove to be a most rewarding task.

(Motivation for Medicine—Paragraph #1)

Comment:

If this is your goal you could become a child care worker or a nursery school teacher. You need to make a reasonable statement about wanting to become a physician. What sets a physician apart from a nursery school teacher? Look at your list of characteristics — is there anything mentioned that's not true of both roles?

> During my previous course work at Midwestern University, I was involved in several extracurricular activities. My participation in these organizations has really been a positive factor in my life because they entailed social interaction with respect to working with others toward a common goal. They also provided an atmosphere in which I was working with others who may or may not have shared my ideas and beliefs. Learning to deal with situations of this nature will prove to be of value throughout my career since the medical profession involves making judgements and decisions based on one's beliefs.

(Extracurricular Activities—Paragraph #2)

Comment:

Other than omitting the details from your first draft you have not addressed the other problems in this paragraph. When you say, ". . . the medical profession involves making judgements and decisions based on one's beliefs" you need to realize that you have identified something that is a part of any career, not just medicine. This type of statement gives your reader the impression that you are naive about what it means to be a physician.

Overall Comment:

You continue to address issues/items that are greater than those which need your attention. This is a Personal Comments page. Your readers want to find out about you other than the what, where and when information in the rest of the application. ***Think*** about what it means to you to have had these experiences. Tell your reader clearly and directly what you mean.

We are repeating the final version of this student's essay to provide greater continuity for your reading. Notice how the essay developed into one that is personalized and interesting to read.

Personal Comments—Final Version

> My decision to seek a career in medicine was influenced by various work and personal experiences. However, there is one person, very dear to me, who played a significant role in finalizing my career objective, my grandmother. Shortly after my twelfth birthday, she was diagnosed as having meningitis and was hospitalized. I can remember having very intense feelings of frustration resulting from the fact that I was unable to care for her. Five days after she had been admitted into the hospital, she went into a coma. At her bedside, I promised her that I would work as hard as I could to become a doctor so that I could help someone get well so they could return home. When she died the following week, I became even more determined than ever to become a physician in hopes of sparing others.
> Over the last nine years my interest in becoming a physician has been strengthened by my extracurricular and work activities. While in high school, I worked as an assistant to a registered pharmacist. My duties consisted of citing pharmacological references which would be incorporated in a monthly newsletter published by the company. As a result of this

exposure, I was able to interpret how various drugs could be used to modify the functions of the autonomic nervous system to alleviate illness. During the summer of 1979, I was a volunteer worker at the hospital, where I processed medical histories for incoming patients, took temperatures, and prepared blood and urine specimens. This was my first "hands on" experience and gave me an idea of some of the intricate workings of a hospital.

While at Midwestern University, my participation in extracurricular activities enhanced my interpersonal and leadership skills. They provided situations in which I was allowed to exercise my capabilities as president, vice president, treasurer and secretary.

I have also been involved in other activities which have given me the opportunity to help those who are socioeconomically disadvantaged and unable to care for themselves. This volunteer work ranged from organizing food drives and establishing a tutor program for primary school children to visiting pediatric wards of hospitals and talking with the children to ease their fears that resulted from being hospitalized. These services were rewarding to me personally because I was able to make a positive change in their lives and, in many cases, become a friend to many that really needed some type of role model. I also worked on the crisis hotline at a local hospital. My responsibilities were to be a very attentive, confident listener and provide the caller with reference information pertinent to the inquiry. Through this experience I have gained confidence in dealing with crisis situations.

During my senior year at Midwestern, I was employed by the United States Department of Agriculture as a Biological Aide. I received, cataloged and analyzed the triglyceride content of seeds shipped from various parts of the United States, thus I worked extensively with nuclear magnetic resonance machines and mass spectroscopy equipment. I also performed bio-assays on the velvet leaf plant. This experience improved my research ability and familiarized me with agricultural methods of mass production. Presently, I am a volunteer autopsy assistant.

My desire to become a physician is sincere and I am committed to doing whatever is necessary to achieve my goal.

The reader now realizes why this person wants to become a physician. Moreover, one is able to see the pattern of work experiences and extracurricular activities that lead toward aspirations of becoming a physician. It is not presented here as a model AMCAS statement; rather it is presented to illustrate how a more personalized statement could evolve.

SAMPLE ESSAYS

We have selected two essays that are representative of sincere, to-the-point statements. We realize there is a possibility you may be tempted to fashion your statement after one of these. That would be a mistake. As you read them, consider the impression you are developing of the writer. When you begin to write your own personal comments, keep your reader(s) in mind and try to determine the impression you are making.

Example of an Effective Personal Comments Page

During my life, I have worn many "hats": student, researcher, medical assistant, drug rehabilitation counselor, EKG technician, insurance clerk, nurse's aid and donut-maker. My most rewarding experiences have been those which provided opportunities to help others in a medical setting.

My first direct exposure to medicine occurred the summer after high school graduation. At that time, I began working as a medical asssitant for a physician. In addition to learning technical skills, such as the procedures for EKG's and chest x-rays, I learned the pleasure and pain of caring for others. The pleasure came when a patient was improved by the physician's careful treatment. The pain came in the heartache of an incurable disease in an old man or in the sudden heart attack of a stranger on the sidewalk.

Although I was keenly interested in medicine, I lacked the self-confidence to pursue a medical career at that time. Since I have always been fascinated by people, my undergraduate major in sociology seemed a natural choice. My post-secondary education took place in a variety of locations. This was due primarily to factors involving my marriage and subsequent divorce. I feel that attending different universities and living in various regions of the country have broadened my perspectives and given me the opportunity to incorporate many regional customs as my own.

After receiving my undergraduate degree, I earned a master's degree in sociology. My interest in medicine remained constant through health-related part-time jobs and a focus on medical sociology in my graduate research. Issues such as drug abuse and attitudes toward death were among my concerns. During my two years of graduate school, I co-authored three publications, six research monographs, and five papers for presentation at professional meetings. In addition, I was sole author of a book review and two papers for presentation at professional meetings.

My interest in pursuing a medical degree was heightened by a unique job experience working with rural elderly. During the summer of 1979, in a needs assessment survey which involved hour-long, in-home interviews with older people about their medical, social, economic and nutritional concerns, I came to the realization that health was their primary concern. My heart went out to them and my desire to provide the elderly with humanistic medical care led me to return to school to pursue the pre-medical requirements. My previous doubts about my abilities to compete as a pre-medical student had been based on the misconception that pre-medical students had more intelligence and drive than I had. However, as I matured, the aura with which I had viewed medicine evaporated and I now knew that I had the capacity to succeed in a medical school curriculum.

My interest in rural primary health care is such that, upon acceptance to medical school, I plan to enter into an agreement with a hospital in Smalltown, U.S.A., which will involve my establishing a practice in Smalltown in return for financial assistance with my medical education. I feel that I bring to medicine a unique set of life experiences, an understanding of society, a sincere interest in helping others, and a strong determination to succeed.

Example of an Effective Personal Comments Page

At the end of my first semester of college, when I first decided on medicine as a career, I did so thinking it to be the best thing I could possibly make of my life. Little of this decision was based upon a factual knowledge of medicine, most of my firsthand impressions of doctors having come from childhood cuts and bruises and adolescent experiences in hospital corridors waiting with my parents as my grandfather was dying of emphysema. Doctors then were people who knew things I couldn't know, things imperative to life, imperative to *my* life and the people I loved. They were messengers from a "someplace else" where the decisions were made and the odds calculated; they seemed in control of events that I wanted very badly to have control of myself. This made them important people, people of vast influence. These were the subconscious impressions which became a conscious decision on the day I first seriously asked myself what I wanted from my future.

Since that time, I've acquired a more realistic view of medicine from my discussions with physicians, professors, nurses and friends now in medical school. I've spent time as an EMT on ambulances, in emergency rooms and in an autopsy room, seeing for myself some of the decisions being made by doctors and the other many health professionals. My sister, an oncology nurse on the West Coast, gave me the chance to see the wards where she works and to discuss cancer treatments and death. For the past two years, I've had weekly experience working with a man afflicted with progressive and severe Multiple Sclerosis. I have worked for two years tutoring learning-disabled students both at the college and junior high levels. Beyond this, I have been employed for the previous year as a student lab assistant in a university medical school observing and interacting with the medical students and staff. From these opportunities and others I've gleaned that the physician's job involves more than the application of intelligence. It is a career which demands tenacity, faith, objectivity and, perhaps more importantly, compassion. It is a profession offering physical as well as mental challenges, direct human-to-human contact when it frequently counts more, a measure of business autonomy and relative prestige. I can never see the job as becoming boring.

Near the end of my sophomore year and throughout my junior year I underwent the breakup of a five-year relationship. It also became apparent at this time that my parents, with three other kids in college, could no longer provide any substantial financial support. My work hours increased to 20, 25 and sometimes 30 per week trying to make ends meet ("What?--Popcorn for supper again?!"). With classes becoming more complex, I found myself incredibly frustrated in my science coursework, due in part to a lack of science preparation in high school and, more importantly, to poorly developed study habits. Against my better instincts, I remained in school for another year, after which I took a year off to travel, make money and study myself. I came back the following year, trying hard to convince myself of an alternative profession but ultimately was unable to give up on medicine as a career choice.

I still believe with the great playwright, George Bernard Shaw, that "ages of faith, of romance, and of science are all driven at last to have but one prayer: 'Make me a healthy animal.'" The physician, I believe serves as the vital role in fulfilling that request. I also agree with—and feel that my record reflects—the philosophy of the not-necessarily-so-great poet, Al Stewart, when he says, "nothing that's real is ever for free and you just have to pay for it sometime." The costs of a medical career are high but I feel the rewards are even greater.

WHAT IMPRESSION DOES YOUR ESSAY CONVEY?

What does a reader learn about an applicant from reading the essay on the Personal Comments page of the AMCAS application? Experienced admissions officers from three medical schools agreed to provide written impressions of the Personal Comments pages of six students. Thus, each essay that follows has responses from two admissions officers. After the responses of the admissions officers you will find a summary statement which should help you understand the impact of the admissions officers' comments.

These responses serve to reinforce a suggestion made earlier: it's impossible to always say "the right thing" or to second-guess your readers. Since you won't be able to cover all the bases, you need to appreciate the fact that a sincere statement will best represent you as an applicant.

Personal Comments—Candidate One

Since elementary school, medicine has appealed to me as a humanistic profession in which individuals can receive assistance for their most important priority in life—their health. There have been times I have wondered, "Is medicine right for me?" In the preceding years I have tested my desire by working in health facilities, by working with troubled children, and by communicating with people who have different goals.

Spending summers working at clinics and nursing homes has taught me the value of respect towards the elderly. It is my hope that as a practicing physician I will be able to improve the delivery and treatment of health care to the elderly patient. My interactions with this population provided me with invaluable experience that will help me comfort and care for the elderly in the future. I also began to realize that by speaking my second language (Spanish) I could provide assistance to Spanish-speaking patients who were in pain and in need of my services to relate their problems to a physician. There is a great need in the inner cities for physicians who can speak Spanish. I will be able to help address this problem by practicing medicine in an area that has this need. In addition to my nursing home experience, I volunteered weekly at an assistance center and worked with disadvantaged children with emotional problems. The need to treat these children with love and understanding provided me with some insight into the world of battered children which physicians face throughout their career.

Extracurricular activities provided me the opportunity to broaden my leadership experience. In M.O.V.E. (Mobilization of Volunteer Effort), I was responsible for soliciting and training volunteers which enabled me to work with other organizations within the University. I also helped coordinate the scheduling of volunteers for two Red Cross blood drives. As vice-president of the campus pre-med club, I scheduled meetings, arranged for guest speakers and publicized events. In the process, I learned that it takes a lot of patience and discipline to meet the responsibilities for organizing group activities.

I have listened to views from individuals involved directly in the medical profession and can appreciate basically how my life would be as a physician. I feel confident that I can meet the daily demands of a medical career and maintain the depth of knowledge necessary to be an effective physician. I plan to apply my second language and feel that the challenge of improving the health care within the Hispanic and elderly community will keep my career enjoyable. Most importantly, as the field of medical science advances, I would like to be a part of those changes while continuing to grow and improve as a physician and individual.

Reader One

This person appears to be service oriented. He/she speaks with warmth and compassion about the elderly and battered children. He/she has taken time to work with emotionally disturbed children and in nursing homes, and I suspect s/he has an understanding of what it would be like to be a health-care provider. Through volunteering and club work he/she appears to have learned to work effectively with others. He/she seems confident and would probably be an effective sensitive physician.

Reader Two

My initial feelings about this candidate are that he/she would not be perceived as very strong and in all likelihood would not be invited for an interview. In reading the application, several questions arose, which were not answered by the statements in the application. Some of my observations are shared below:

1. The student appears to have had limited experiences and minimal leadership activities.
2. It is difficult to determine if the student has had any stressful life experiences, and whether under pressure the student would be sufficiently resourceful and/or able to cope.
3. The student appears to be sincere and goal oriented in his/her motivation for medicine. The extent to which naivete exists is not readily apparent through the type of comments which have been shared.
4. The student does not appear to be a risk-taker. The commentary is so general that questions arise as to whether there is a strong intention to please.
5. The ego stability appears to be solid enough from the minimal amount of information shared, but it would be helpful to know if this student had some insight into academic reserve, and whether or not if the person got into trouble, s/he would be able to seek help.
6. The student does not really develop any understanding for the reader as to how or why Spanish has become a second language. There is no clue as to Hispanic identity or involvement either through extracurricular activities or classwork. One can only take on face value that what the student says is true. If this were a really important part of the selection process for an admissions committee, conducting the interview in Spanish might be helpful.
7. The personal statement, in general, is very non-revealing. It would appear that the student is not very adept at conveying insights about himself/herself, or in convincing the reader about what was gained through personal experiences.

Summary Statement

Reader one seems sufficiently satisfied that the applicant demonstrated understanding of the characteristics necessary for health care delivery and as a consequence, would be an effective, sensitive physician.

On the other hand, the second reader felt the statement raised more questions than it answered. Therefore, suggestions were made by the second reader that would have been helpful if answered. Since the readers' comments were not in total agreement, the applicant may experience some feeling of helplessness concerning the ability to satisfy different readers. Again, we remind you that you must make a sincere statement. One has to be satisfied with taking small steps during the application process to professional schools. One small step is your assurance that the personal statement best represents you as an applicant.

Personal Comments—Candidate Two

Several factors have contributed to my decision to become a physician. Throughout my life, I have been given opportunities to assume responsibility, develop discipline, help others, and pursue goals. My parents have been very influential in my progression in all of these areas. As a young person, I was given various chores which carried with them responsibilities. Living on a small farm in a rural area has afforded several opportunities to work both independently and collectively with others. Growing up in a small town has also made me aware of and sensitive to the needs of the people of a small community. My parents have instilled in me the importance of being both genuinely concerned about others and willing to contribute whatever talents or abilities I possess to help those around me. While in high school and college, I actively participated in various athletic programs. I found my experiences in athletics to be very beneficial in developing discipline. I not only learned to be physically disciplined, but I also became disciplined in the maximum utilization of my time. I find now that physical activity is still an asset to a well-rounded lifestyle. Perhaps the most valuable of my parents' contribution has been their unlimited encouragement.

Along with my family's influence, my educational interests were also factors which contributed to my decision to pursue a career in medicine. Throughout high school, I had a strong interest in science; that interest has grown throughout my college years even though I found other areas to be valuable as well. While attending college, I have followed a pre-medical curriculum and have acquired a solid foundation in the basics of biology, chemistry, and physics. As noted on my academic record, however, I received below average grades in the second semester of organic chemistry, and, therefore, I do intend to take the second semester of organic chemistry again in the spring and obtain a satisfactory grade.

In addition to my science background, I feel I have gained a broad perspective of other areas of study. During the 1982 fall semester, I participated as a member of a research team in the Department of Psychology studying the relationship between sleep patterns and headaches. I have also expanded my knowledge of the humanities by taking courses such as music, literature, and sociology. In taking these courses, I have developed a deeper appreciation for the unique qualities that contribute to any individual's dedication to those fields.

Additional factors have served to reinforce my decision to become a physician. One of those factors has been my exposure to several aspects of patient care and interaction. In 1983, while attending summer school, I worked as a volunteer in the V.A. Medical Center Pharmacy. This afforded me the opportunity to be in contact with several patients. More recently, after receiving my certification as an Emergency Medical Technician (EMT), I have been working for the local Fire Department's Ambulance Service. My work as an EMT has not only given me an opportunity to provide emergency care and deal with patients and their families in the field, but also to assist and, most importantly, observe in the emergency room. The experiences I have had while providing emergency care have been some of the most challenging yet rewarding of my life. My work in this field has contributed greatly to my desire to become a physician.

Perhaps one of the strongest motivating factors for my desire to become a physician is my awareness of the need for physicians in my hometown and even more generally in this area. There is a definite need for physicians to not only establish their practices but also to make a commitment to remain in the community and become actively involved beyond the realm of medicine. It is my plan to return to this area and establish a reputation of having both a medical practice and a personal lifestyle that does, indeed, serve the community.

Reader One

This young person professes an interest in and concern for others, but gives little evidence of activities to support his/her contentions. He/she calls attention to club, research, EMT and E.R. activities, but does not speak of the ***people*** with whom he/she came into contact. He/she may be "people oriented," but it does not come across in the essay. His/Her motivation seems to be to fill a need for physicians in the community and may not derive from within. Although he/she has had numerous opportunities to observe the delivery of health care, he/she does not speak of a single patient or of deriving personal satisfaction from participation in assisting them. I have reservations regarding his/her sensitivity to others and understanding of what life will be like as a physician.

Reader Two

While this student appears to be a bonafide rural student and a type of student we would be interested in, there are aspects of the application which raise some questions:

1. The Personal Statement is not a very revealing one. The student demonstrates little depth or insight regarding personal experiences. It would be important to know whether or not there is an ability to integrate information from various experiences, including academics, in order to be a problem solver of sufficient depth in order to succeed in medicine.
2. The motivation appears genuine and is based on experiences. The choice of rural medicine appears to be based on living in that type of setting and deriving pleasure from the people, but also in recognizing a real need.

Summary Statement

The readers' comments in this case are similar. Simply put, if you raise issues you should be certain to clarify and support those issues. Discussing issues in a general fashion will not suffice. As an example, both readers were concerned that the applicant did not have a realistic perception of his/her ability to handle a medical curriculum. Moreover, the driving force to become a physician seemed to be extrinsically motivated—the need for physicians in a rural setting rather than a personal sense of commitment and an ability to perform well in medical school. The caution here is to raise and resolve a few issues clearly rather than generally covering a number of issues.

The medical profession combines knowledge and wisdom from just about every aspect of life which is directed towards helping humanity. A physician is not just part of the health care team but the leader of the health care team. He is free to practice broadly or to acquire a specialty of his own choosing. Thus medicine offers the challenges and fulfillment that I am seeking in a career.

Growing up on the farm and taking part in farm related tasks at a very early age have instilled in me a great deal of responsibility. For example I started driving tractors when I was five years old. When I was in high school I was a member of Future Farmers of America and I farmed my own plot of land. I was in control of all financial and production aspects of it. Consequently, before most people were getting their first jobs I was already taking on a great amount of responsibility on the farm. With my farm background it makes it very easy to relate to people from rural areas. Farming combines many skills related to science and mechanical technologies. Working with and repairing farm equipment have enabled me to develop good manipulative skills with my hands.

It was in high school that I first seriously considered becoming a physician. A physician came to one of our classes where he told us the good and bad aspects of medicine as a profession. He also told us what would be expected of us in college to get into medical school. That same day a pharmacist came in and told us about pharmacy as a profession and how pharmacy and medicine used to be one profession. I decided the best possible undergraduate degree to prepare myself for medicine would be pharmacy. I entered college with a prepharmacy major in 1977. After two years of prepharmacy I was accepted into pharmacy school. It was hard going all the way through pharmacy school when I knew that my ultimate goal was to become a physician. I think that in the end it has helped me become a much better candidate for medical school. I have learned to be able to process and master large quantities of material including medical books and journals. I have been conditioned to develop self-discipline. I think that these are two important qualities a medical student should have.

In my last year of pharmacy school I had mostly clinical rotations. It was during this period of time that I knew that being a physician was my greatest desire in life. In these clinical rotations I worked side by side with medical students and medical residents in deciding on drug therapies for their patients. I made rounds and went to staffings with medical students and medical residents. I spent hours talking to patients on a one-to-one basis answering questions about the drugs they were taking and being concerned about their illnesses. There was one patient who had necrosing vasculitis for which I spent many hours outside of class time searching literature for new therapies for vasculitis. I was encouraged by the many medical students and physicians who told me that I would make a good physician.

During my undergraduate education I worked as an EMTA for two local ambulance services and also as a pharmacy apprentice. During the time I worked I had a great opportunity to interact with many people. Being an EMTA provided close contact with the medical profession. I really enjoyed my work as an EMTA and working with sick people.

After I graduated I decided to work for two years to pay my bills and save money for medical school. Also, I thought it would be a good idea to see if I couldn't be satisfied with the practice of pharmacy as a profession. I worked for two years as a staff pharmacist. I found out what I knew to be true already. There just isn't enough patient contact in pharmacy for me. Drug therapies are just a small aspect of the practice of medicine. I want to learn about diagnosis and other non-drug therapies as well.

Reader One

This student appears to be somewhat egocentric and perhaps insensitive to others or even arrogant. His/her motivation for medicine may be more to achieve status and power than to attend the sick. He/she appears to have little insight into the demands of health care delivery. I am concerned about his/her ability to interact with others in a mutually satisfying and effective manner. He/she would probably be a rather ineffective, frustrated physician.

Reader Two

In several places this essay does not ring true. It leaves the reader with more questions than answers. The information in the opening paragraph is such common knowledge that its presentation serves no purpose. The second paragraph would be more effective if the author mentioned specific accomplishments. As it is, the reader is left with the unsettling image of a five year old driving a tractor and wonders if there is some exaggeration here.

In the third paragraph the explanation of why the author decided to enter pharmacy school does not make much sense, and this contributes to the artificial tone of the essay. Later in the essay, when the author states that he/she worked as a pharmacist for two years to see if he/she would be satisfied with the profession, he/she contradicts himself/herself. The reader is left with the impression that the author is not being totally honest.

Although most of the writing in the essay is mechanically correct, there are some awkward constructions. The final sentence seems tacked on to fill the available space and weakens the organization. The author does not seem to have planned the essay in advance or spent much time on revision.

Summary Statement

There are too many "I" statements in this application. As such, one reader thought the writer egocentric or arrogant. The concern, therefore, is how does one balance responsibility and accomplishment and not seem egocentric. A clue is provided in the response of reader one. Balancing specific accomplishments directly related to medicine would indicate knowledge and awareness of the demands of health care delivery. Also, instead of discussing personal accomplishments in the treatment of a patient, the applicant could have discussed satisfaction from the patient's viewpoint. Instead of personalizing the essay, as was the applicant's intent, the applicant was perceived by one reader as being arrogant and the other as being insincere. The writer must be able to balance personal achievements with a sense of direction and humility.

Personal Comments—Candidate Four

After my mother was diagnosed as having emphysema 14 years ago, I often accompanied her on her clinical visits and was befriended by the physicians who treated her. In effect, they introduced me to medicine; I was permitted to listen with a stethoscope to my mother's breathing patterns, go to the laboratories, and see and hear explanations of many aspects of her disease. Fascinated with the functions of the human pulmonary system, I strove to learn more by reading books and participating in school-sponsored science fairs. A few years later, my stepfather developed arteriosclerosis and my interests broadened to include cardiovascular diseases. I pursued my interest in the medical field in high school by achieving an award of distinction in biology and participating in pre-medical programs offered to students at local hospitals.

The stability of my mother's health during my first years in college allowed me to concentrate on my studies and establish a good academic record. I transferred to West Coast University because it offered a more thorough biological science education and numerous medical internship opportunities. It was also close enough to San Francisco so I could get home easily when my mother needed me. The summer was spent in an Emergency Medical Technician training and certification course. I had the opportunity to work at the county hospital where most of the patients were low-income minorities with backgrounds similar to my own. Working as an EMT made me realize that there is a severe need for minority doctors in poorer urban areas.

During my last two years of college, I encountered financial difficulties which required my working 20+ hours a week. I was employed by a university-run program designed to encourage and motivate minority students to seek a university education. Unfortunately, the effects of working and taking care of my mother as she battled her on-going illness with frequent hospital stays are reflected in my transcript.

Also while an undergraduate I participated in an internship at the Department of Family Practice of the university's medical center where I saw a diverse group of patients. I also developed a good rapport with both patients and doctors which allowed me the opportunity to observe and assist in various clinical examinations that most other volunteers were not permitted to do.

My primary interest in cardiopulmonary function was extended when I volunteered as a student research assistant. The professor's research on hypertension happened to coincide with my mother's developing of high blood pressure due to her respiratory difficulties. This experience broadened my interest in the medical field by introducing me to biomedical research. After graduation, I was chosen to participate in a special program at a research laboratory. I worked on a team investigating the effects of calcium channel blockers on experimentally induced liver damage in rats. The results from my project were exciting because we observed an inhibitory trend in calcium channel blockers against liver damaging agents. My project, along with further studies conducted after my internship, was invited for formal presentation at the American Gastroenterology Association meeting and is currently being edited for publication. I was also selected to go to the National Institutes of Health to participate in the Normal Volunteer program. While in Bethesda, I was involved in histochemical research determining the protein composition of various human and bovine brain tumors and in conducting neurological studies in rats.

During this time I applied to medical school for the next entering class. I was placed on alternate lists by four schools but I did not matriculate. I was very disappointed since I felt I was ready for medical school. Everything has a purpose however, because my mother died in October of that next year and I was thankful that I was able to be with her when she needed me most.

After a year of postbaccalaureate work I feel stronger and academically it shows in my record. I am on track and am confident that my efforts and experience demonstrate my commitment to study medicine and become a physician.

Reader One

This student is someone that we would definitely invite for an interview. There is a high degree of vigor in this person that comes through in the Personal Comment. There is a sense of someone who enjoys life, who is willing to risk, who has things to be accomplished, has good initiative, and who will get where he/she wants to go with hard work, determination and enthusiasm. These assessments would need to be confirmed through the interview, as well as clarification of the following:

1. Even though this student did not fully detail what was learned through personal experiences, there is a fair amount conveyed in the Personal Comment. Interview questions would be directed toward the number of activities, and the degree to which he/she felt they interfered with greater success in the sciences. I would be interested in determining what was learned about priority setting.
2. I would be interested in knowing how this student has considered financing his/her medical education. The exploration would be to determine how realistic the plan is, and whether there is an understanding about how much work can be done along with the medical school curriculum.

Reader Two

This essay is an instance of an author referring in some detail to a painful personal experience, the death of his/her mother. Such essays can be difficult to evaluate, particularly if the author relies too much on the personal experience as an excuse for failure to do well. For the most part, I think the author of this essay avoids this problem. There is enough information about solid accomplishments (EMT training, research, NIH work, and alternate list status) to balance the explanation of academic difficulties. More information should have been given about the Family Practice internship. It is unwise for an author to say he/she was given special opportunities without specifying why and what they are. The discussion of the previous application is clear and well done. The entire essay gives the impression that the author made a serious effort to communicate with the reader.

Summary Statement

There is a general statement that this applicant wrote with conviction. While there are yet questions that need to be answered, it is clear that the statement was written with the intention to communicate. In this case, the applicant was able to discuss difficult life experiences and yet not seem to use those experiences as excuses.

Personal Comments—Candidate Five

I don't remember making a conscious decision to become a physician; it was as if I were born with an affinity for medicine. For as long as I can remember I have possessed an extremely strong interest in the field of health care which manifested itself through my early education. Excelling through grammar and high school was a direct result of my early commitment to learn. Although my family was financially disadvantaged, hard work and determination made it possible for me to attend college. My years spent at school were enriched by the competitiveness and drive for excellence of my peers. It was necessary that I work hard in order to reach and then surpass the level of those who had been blessed with a better high school education.

My interest in medicine was strengthened by two factors, both of which I consider to be of utmost importance. The first is that I have deep concern and compassion for people. While in high school I served as a tutor for a couple of hours each week at the community center. I would assist neighborhood children who had problems with various subjects, such as math, science or English. I was also a tutor to other high school students who didn't pick up subjects, such as calculus or trigonometry, as rapidly as I did. I have always been willing to lend a helping hand, and have always been able to work well with others. It is through my help to others that I gain a sense of satisfaction. Secondly, it is my love of science that reinforces the interest I have in medicine. Science, by its very nature, lends itself to intrigue and intellectual stimulation. My fascination with it has and will always leave me with a thirst for knowledge.

Spending time with my cousin, a practicing surgeon, helped me realize that becoming a physician is a demanding profession. It requires decision making, competency, motivation, extreme dedication, compassion and an orientation toward lifelong learning. The exposure I have had to applied health has served to reassure me that I have made the correct career choice. I have gained an understanding of rewards and problems of working with the sick. Volunteer work at a local hospital was a rewarding experience. I was able to not only be of service to the sick but also to supplement knowledge gained in the classroom. I also served as a volunteer at a health assessment center. My duties included treating minor ailments, taking blood pressures, measuring percent of body fat, distributing literature on health and medically related topics, and giving advice on where to seek further help.

After the birth of my daughter I thought it best to spend two years away from school during an important developmental stage of her life. Upon returning to school, my objectives were to strengthen my science academic background and prepare for the Medical College Admissions Test.

I am aware of the need for physicians in medically underserved areas. By no choice of their own, people of these areas have had to suffer the effects of living where there is insufficient medical personnel to care for the needs of the region. The medical profession has the responsibility for the medical care of every individual in society. My hope is that in the near future more of these underserved areas will have sufficient medical personnel. Health professionals must work together to increase the medical services in these areas and also to improve the quality of health care available to society. I would like to be in a position to one day work with other medical doctors and health care professionals for the betterment of society through the delivery of quality health care.

Reader One

This woman took time to do a number of volunteer activities to help others and apparently derives satisfaction from these activities. Through these activities she appears to have gained some insight into the lifestyle she would live as a physician. She expresses strong motivation and a desire to provide health care in underserved areas. As a physician she would probably be a caring patient advocate.

Reader Two

This essay is well organized and thus easy to read. The author introduces each paragraph with a clear topic sentence. The writing is mechanically correct. Obviously, this is not a first draft but rather the result of planning and revision.

Although the author occasionally makes statements that are so common in application essays that they have become cliches (*e.g.,* being born with an interest in medicine, wanting to become a doctor out of a desire to help others and a love of science), the essay succeeds in creating a vivid impression on the reader because it is full of specific details that make the statements sound genuine. The author specifies what she did as a tutor, what she did working with her cousin and volunteering at the health service. The reference to other people by name helps shift the focus away from the author at times. In addition to providing factual information, the author also indicates what important lessons she learned from her experiences. All of these factors make the conclusion of the essay sound appropriate and genuine.

Summary Statement

The ability to include specific details in the personal statement in a succinct manner is important. Including specific details helps paint a clearer, genuine picture. In addition, the applicant, through the use of detail, listed several health-related, people-oriented activities and described lessons learned as a result.

Personal Comment—Candidate Six

My motivation for a career in medicine has developed over a number of years. The driving force for this pursuit is the sincere feeling that medicine allows me to utilize both my strengths and interests in a combination that will be mutually beneficial to myself and others. I enjoy and thrive on the interactions between people, the reasoning and mental stimulation of solving problems, and the satisfaction which comes from my helping others.

While attending public school, I participated in the gifted education curriculum. This program encouraged me and aided with the administrative problems that allowed attendance at my local community college at night and summers during my sophomore and junior years, and half-days during my senior year. I was, thus, able to graduate with an Associate's of Arts degree in one year of full-time study.

Over the past ten years, I have been involved in breeding, training, and showing horses. As a result, I have developed patience and responsibility. The daily feeding and training of the livestock developed self-discipline and responsibility for my actions. In showing my livestock, I developed the ability to work under pressure without conveying my apprehension. In addition, I also learned to accept defeat graciously.

I have received exposure to various facets of the medical profession through volunteering at my local hospital. I was able to observe radiological readings and other activities of a small hospital lab and emergency room. More recently, I have volunteered with the Women's Center as a pregnancy counselor. This work involves one-to-one contact with the women who utilize these services. I have further increased my interest in counseling work through this experience.

My work as a Teaching Assistant and Resident Advisor contributed to my interests in becoming involved with a career that allows greater and more diverse interpersonal contacts. Both of these employment opportunities entailed the task of being presented with a problem or a very puzzled student and sitting down with him or her to explain and/or solve the problem. This exposure, subsequently, enhanced my growth in verbal reasoning and interpersonal communication.

At Midwestern University, I have become involved with a research project on the problem of desulfurizing coal. My assignment is to assist with analyzing Mossbauer spectrum and to develop and to modify existing programs which use the least square method to mathematically fit the spectrum. In addition, I have worked with microcomputers and other electronic instruments since early high school. I am familiar with several languages and basic electronics. I am very excited about the integration of technology into medicine and I am actively trying to become literate in these areas.

I have also pursued a small research study on the cognitive process skills of the MCAT. This independent project researched the question of what the MCAT is actually demanding in the way of thought processes. I used Bloom's Taxonomy of Cognitive Skills and Science Process Skills to categorize questions in the MCAT manual in the areas of Science Problems and Quantitative Skills.

I am presently pursuing a degree in chemistry while increasing my exposure and knowledge of the biological sciences. Throughout my education, I have been exposed to excellent instructors who have deepened and broadened my learning experiences in the basic areas of science and allowed me to have further exposure to the medical field and medical education.

Reader One

This student appears to be a solid academic performer while carrying a fair number of work hours concurrently. He/she is someone we would choose to interview, however, there are a number of questions that would be asked in the interview. I have listed those below:

1. I think it was commendable of this student to take an AA degree with one additional year of coursework following high school at a junior college, but by doing this, did he/she really aim lower than he/she should have? If he/she were identified and participated in a gifted curriculum, shouldn't he/she have been encouraged to seek a challenging college *following* his/her high school? This would lead me to look at this student's overall ability to take risks.
2. While the student professes strong interest in people and that serves as his/her primary motivating force to choose medicine, on balance, more of his/her activities are non-people oriented. I would be interested in listening carefully to what this student says about people and the interactions that he/she has had.
3. I would be interested in the influence of the student's family, particularly in shaping motivation and ability to risk. In many respects, the statements about motivation are quite standard, and I would want to know how insightful the student is, what depth and breadth does he/she have to his/her own thinking, and how he/she has determined his/her own level of commitment necessary to pursue medicine.
4. It is difficult to know whether this student is a leader. I would explore this in the interview, particularly his/her self-perceptions. This would also help me know how much of a risk-taker he/she is. My initial impressions are that he/she is not a leader.
5. Why does this student always attend summer school? Is he/she a compulsive overachiever? Is this why he/she chose to study the MCAT? It is interesting that he/she would choose to look into this, and my interest would be in determining why.

Reader Two

This essay creates a favorable impression because it is organized and correctly written. The author has taken the time to plan and revise the essay, and the reader will appreciate this effort.

I find two general problems with this essay. First, the focus is almost totally on the author. There is no mention of other people and, in some places, a failure to specify what the author actually accomplished or learned through involvement in an activity. The author appears egotistical and unable or unwilling to acknowledge that all experiences are not equally important or successful. This leads to the second problem, a lack of specific information in key places. The author does not indicate what was done in the Women's Center, what was accomplished in the research on coal, what was learned in the study of the MCAT. This lack of detail makes the essay sound like many other application essays, and the impression the essay creates is likely to vanish soon after it has been read. The most successful essays develop a few ideas in sufficient detail to give the reader a vivid impression of the author's personality.

Summary Statement

Both readers agreed that the applicant has written a good essay. There are two factors that seem important from their comments. One factor is not stated and the other is. What was not said was that the reader should note the number of additional questions well-written essays generate. In other words, many essays are so bland that they do not encourage the reader to become involved with the essay. As a consequence, the reader doesn't care to know more. On the other hand, well written essays tend to generate additional questions for interviews. What was said by the second reader also bears repeating—develop a few ideas in sufficient detail. By doing so, readers will get a clear impression of the applicant.

From the readers' points of view and our own, it is important that the personal statements generate enthusiasm for the reader. In order to do so, the applicant must use specific vivid details that describe experiences and lessons learned as a result of the experiences. The applicant must strike a balance between the "I" statements used and, at the same time, convey a sense of accomplishment. Our best advice to attain these tasks is to be sincere, describe a few experiences in detail, rewrite, rewrite, and rewrite until you are convinced that your personal statement describes you as you are as opposed to guessing what some reader wants you to be.

SUPPLEMENTAL APPLICATIONS

Those applicants that meet the initial criteria of a school, minimal GPA, MCAT scores, and residency requirements, are generally sent supplemental applications. The supplemental applications are usually the second step in the admissions process. The supplementals provide another means of reducing the volume of applications. In some cases, the supplemental applications are used to determine whether applicants will be granted a face-to-face interview. The supplementals provide an opportunity to respond to a number of questions. For example, applicants to the medical school at Southern Illinois University are asked to demonstrate how they identify with the purpose of Southern Illinois University. Other questions ask the applicants to discuss their humanities backgrounds and their ability to communicate.

Once the supplemental application is returned to the admissions office at Southern Illinois University, a subcommittee of the admissions committee evaluates the application according to three criteria: Is the application well organized and well written? Does the applicant provide convincing identification with the purpose of the School of Medicine? Should the applicant be invited for an interview? If two of the three screeners agree the applicant is invited for face-to-face interviews. Although the supplemental process is not the same at all medical schools, the obvious errors to avoid in the supplemental process are the same regardless of the procedure used.

Students should take the time to organize a coherent, error-free response. The same caveats that apply to the original application hold for the supplemental application. There is no reason why an applicant should not ask for assistance in preparation of the supplemental application. Remember this application is part of a reduction process. At each step of the process, the applicant is in competition with all other applicants.

Types of Questions Asked

The essay questions posed on supplemental applications vary from school to school. Some schools give you the opportunity to "use this space to address anything else you feel the admissions committee should consider in reviewing your application."

Other schools want you to be much more specific and ask you to address something like, "Discuss a problem you encountered in your undergraduate education and describe how you dealt with it."

There is one question common to many supplementals: "Why have you chosen our medical school?" A good answer to this question necessitates some investigation. The more specifically you can refer to the school the better. Reading the school's catalog is a start. Consider what the school has to offer in terms of how you will be trained to be a physician. If possible, talk to some medical students or faculty members to get a "feel" for the school.

Preparing Your Answers

In our experience, the greatest difficulty that students have in answering questions on supplemental applications is not answering the question which was asked. These students have an agenda of their own which they seem to be determined to address. Thus, they manipulate the question to be able to make the points they're intent on making. This often takes the form of making references to health-related matters when, in reality, a direct answer to the question does not necessitate any reference to medicine.

For example, the school asks you to "describe your most significant accomplishments and experiences and how you achieved them." It is not necessary for these accomplishments and experiences to have anything to do with medicine. You should feel comfortable talking about whatever you consider "your most significant accomplishments and experiences."

After you have drafted your essays, let someone you consider knowledgeable and trustworthy read them. Your reader's responsibility is to give you feedback about the clarity and appropriateness of your statements.

CONCLUSION

Preparing a professional school application is a challenge. You will have a greater chance of meeting the challenge if you are well informed and if you permit yourself enough time to develop your written comments and carefully attend to all the details involved in the process.

We hope you have found our suggestions helpful and, when you endure and persist with your writing you will be successful.

NOTES

NOTES

ACADEMIC RECORD

AMCAS USE ONLY

SSN		
000-00-0000		

LAST NAME	FIRST NAME	MIDDLE NAME	SUFFIX
Doe	John	Andrew	

COLLEGE / LOCATION	ACADEMIC STATUS	BCPM/A	ACADEMIC YEAR	TERM	COURSE NAME	NUMBER	TYPE	OFFICIAL TRANSCRIPT GRADE	SEMESTER HOURS ATTEMPTED	AMCAS GRADE	AMCAS USE
Midwestern University Anytown, USA	FR	C	80	S1	Intro. General Chem.	115		B	3	B	
		A			Regional Geog. of US	255		B	3	B	
		A			English Composition	101		A	3	A	
		M			Col. Algebra and Trig.	111		C	5	C	
		M		S2	Calculus I	150		A	4	A	
		A			Intro. to Art	101		A	3	A	
		C			Intro. to Chem. Princ.	222A		A	4	A	
		B			Intro. to Zoology	118		A	4	A	
		C	81	SS	Intro. to Chem. Princ.	222B		A	4	A	
		A			Nutritional Ecology	236		A	2	A	
	SO	C	81	S1	Organic Chemistry	344		A	4	A	
		C			Lab Technique (Organ.)	345		A	2	A	
		B			Div. Ani. Life-Invert.	220A		A	4	A	
		A			Expository Writing	117		B	2	B	
		A			Intro. to Psychology	202		A	3	A	
		B	81	S2	Genetic-Class Molec.	305		B	3	B	
		C			Organic Chemistry	346		A	2	A	
		C			Lab Technique (Organ.)	347		A	3	A	
		A			Racquetball	104M		A	2	A	
		A			Interpersonal Comm.	152		A	2	A	
		B			Div. Ani. Life-Vert.	220B		A	4	A	
		A			Indiv. Project (Psyc.)	392		A	2	A	
	JR	A	82	SS	Psyc. of Personality	305		A	3	A	
		P		S1	University Physics	205A		C	3	C	
		A			Social Psychology	307		A	3	A	
		B			Developmental Biol.	309		A	3	A	
		B			Element Human Phsl.	210		A	5	A	
		P			University Phys. Lab	255A		A	1	A	
		B		S2	General Botany	200		A	3	A	
		A			Prob. in Philosophy	102		A	3	A	
		P			College Physics	203B		B	3	B	
		P			College Physics Lab	253B		A	1	A	
		B			General Botany Lab	201		A	1	A	
		B			Survey Human Anatomy	301		A	4	A	
	SR	B	83	S1	Survey of Biochem.	450	CC		4		
		B			Princ. of Micro.	301	CC		4		
		B			Botany-Plant Div.	204	CC		3		
		B			Botany-Plant Div. Lab	205	CC		1		
		A			Child Psychology	301	CC		3		
		B		S2	General Microbiology	302	CC		3		